Garden
Friends

FIRST EDITION
Series Editor Deborah Lock; **Senior Art Editor** Tory Gordon-Harris;
Design Assistant Sadie Thomas; **US Editor** Elizabeth Hester;
Pre-Production Producer Nadine King; **Producer** Sara Hu; **Jacket Designer** Natalie Godwin;
Publishing Manager Bridget Giles; **Reading Consultant** Linda Gambrell, PhD

THIS EDITION
Editorial Management by Oriel Square
Produced for DK by WonderLab Group LLC
Jennifer Emmett, Erica Green, Kate Hale, *Founders*

Editors Grace Hill Smith, Libby Romero, Michaela Weglinski;
Photography Editors Kelley Miller, Annette Kiesow, Nicole DiMella;
Managing Editor Rachel Houghton; **Designers** Project Design Company;
Researcher Michelle Harris; **Copy Editor** Lori Merritt; **Indexer** Connie Binder;
Proofreader Larry Shea; **Reading Specialist** Dr. Jennifer Albro;
Curriculum Specialist Elaine Larson

Published in the United States by DK Publishing
1745 Broadway, 20th Floor, New York, NY 10019

A catalog record for this book
is available from the Library of Congress.
HC ISBN: 978-0-7440-6656-2
PB ISBN: 978-0-7440-6655-5

DK books are available at special discounts when purchased
in bulk for sales promotions, premiums, fundraising, or
educational use. For details, contact: DK Publishing Special Markets,
1745 Broadway, 20th Floor, New York, NY 10019
SpecialSales@dk.com

Printed and bound in China

The publisher would like to thank the following for their kind permission to reproduce their images:
a=above; c=center; b=below; l=left; r=right; t=top; b/g=background

123RF.com: Eric Isselee / isselee 5b; **Dorling Kindersley:** Peter Anderson / RHS Hampton Court Flower Show 2014 4-5t;
Dreamstime.com: Eric Isselee 31clb, Lindavostrovska 14br, 15b; **Shutterstock.com:** hwongcc 29bl, 29br, iamharin 4c,
irin-k 10-11b, LapaiIrKrapai 30, SNEHIT PHOTO 6-7

All other images © Dorling Kindersley

For the curious
www.dk.com

Garden Friends

butterfly

garden

Meet the small animals in the garden.

praying mantis

antennae

flower

butterflies

Hello, butterfly.
You are resting
on a flower.

wing

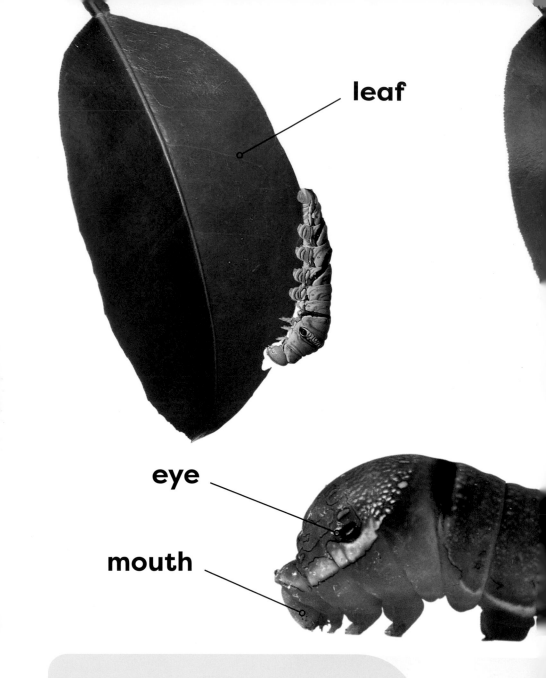

leaf

eye

mouth

caterpillars

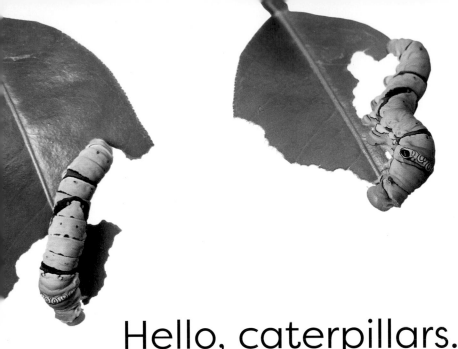

Hello, caterpillars.
You are eating
big leaves.

spot

 **ladybugs**

Hello, ladybugs.
You have
many spots.

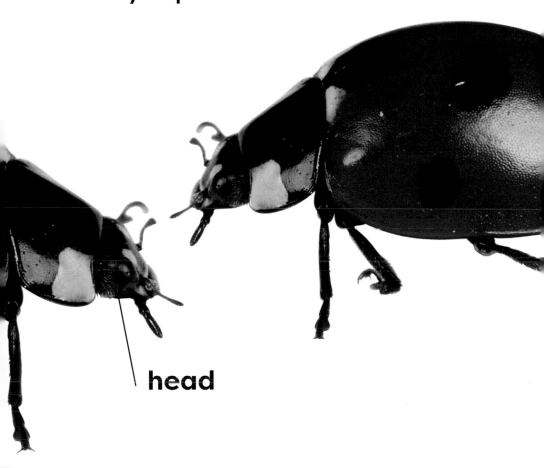

head

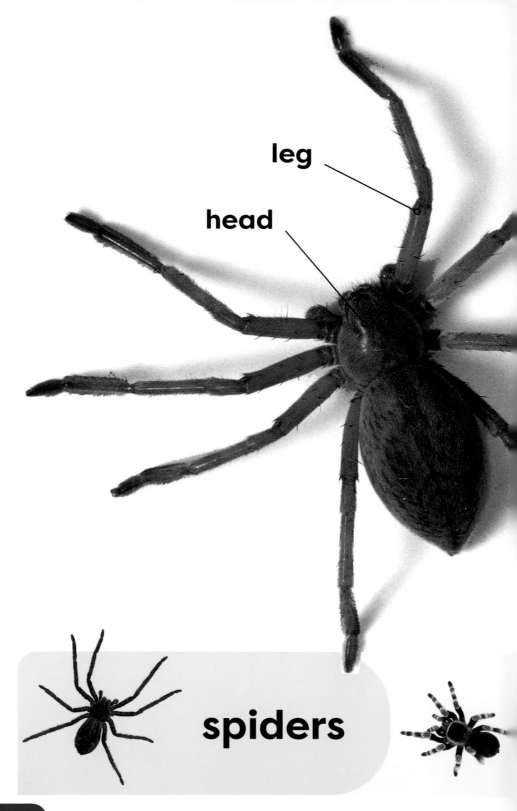

leg

head

spiders

Hello, spider.
You have spun
a big web.

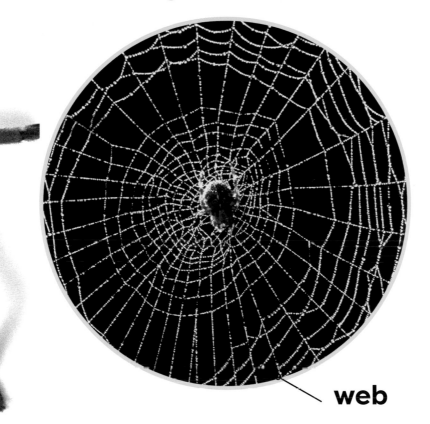

web

flower

furry body

 bumblebees

Hello, bumblebee.
You are drinking
from a flower.

Hello, centipede.
You have many legs.

centipedes

head

leg

Hello, dragonfly.
You are flying
around very fast.

dragonflies

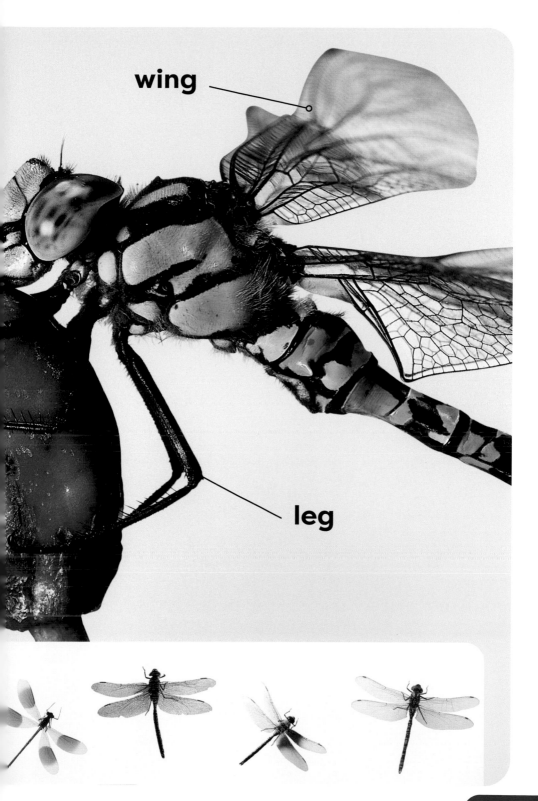

wing

leg

baby snail

shell

snails

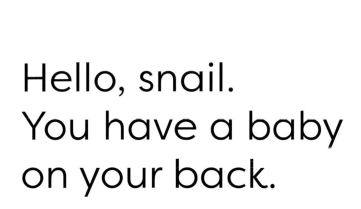

Hello, snail.
You have a baby
on your back.

soft body

worms

Hello, worms.
You are very long.

Hello, stag beetle.
You have very
sharp jaws.

wing

beetles

head

jaws

Hello, frogs.
You are hiding
in the grass.

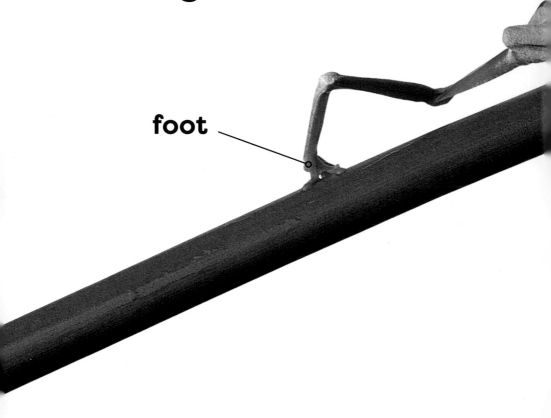

foot

frogs

grasshoppers

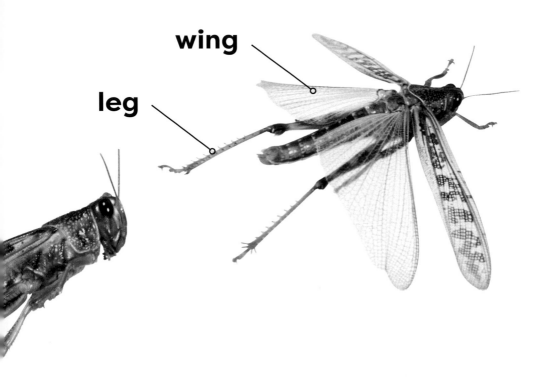

wing

leg

Hello, grasshoppers.
Wow!
What a big jump!

What animals can you find outside?

Glossary

antennae
are used by insects to
feel their surroundings

centipede
an insect with
many legs

jaws
are used by stag beetles
to fight and nip

praying mantis
a bright green insect
with long front legs

web
something that some
spiders make to catch
prey and rest

Quiz

Answer the questions to see what you have learned. Check your answers with an adult.

Which animal am I?

1. I have many spots.

2. I drink from flowers.

3. I have very sharp jaws.

4. I have a soft body.

5. I move around by taking big jumps.

1. A ladybug 2. A bumblebee 3. A stag beetle
4. A worm 5. A grasshopper